TRICKY RIDDLES

O N SMITH

L R RUGGERI

Hello, my name is Ridley. This book contains 300 riddles and loads of challenges!

I will give you 10 riddles followed by the answers on the next page. Have a sneak peek if you find them too tricky

Enjoy my tricky riddles!

1. What has keys but can't open locks?

2. What has a head, a tail, but no body?

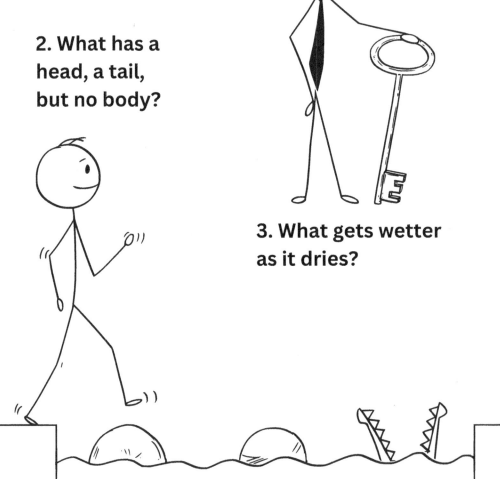

3. What gets wetter as it dries?

4. What has many teeth but can't bite?

5. What is full of holes but still holds water?

6. What has one eye but can't see?

7. What can travel around the world while staying in a corner?

8.What dress can you not wear?

9. What has hands but can't clap?

10. What has a thumb and four fingers but is not alive?

ANSWERS

1. A piano

2. A coin

3. A towel

4. A comb

5. A sponge

6. A needle

7. A stamp

8. An address

9. A clock

10. A glove

CHALLENGE

What 4-letter word can be written
forward, backward, or upside down,
and can still be read from left to right?

11. What is always in front of you but can't be seen?

12. What has a neck but no head?

13. What has cities but no houses, forests but no trees, and rivers but no water?

14. What is not alive but grows, doesn't have lungs but needs air, and doesn't have a mouth but needs water?

15. What runs but never walks, has a bed but never sleeps, and can be found in both the city and country?

16. What is light as a feather, yet the strongest person can't hold it for much longer than a minute?

17. What is always coming but never arrives?

18.What has a bottom at the top?

19. What comes once in a minute, twice in a moment, but never in a thousand years?

20. What goes up but never comes...

...down?

ANSWERS

11. The future

16. Your breath

12. A bottle

17. Tomorrow

13. A map

18. A leg

14. A fire

19. The letter 'M'

15. A river

20. Your age

CHALLENGE

How many times can you subtract the
number two from the number fifty?

Once. After that you're subtracting it from 48.

21. What is white when it's dirty and black when it's clean?

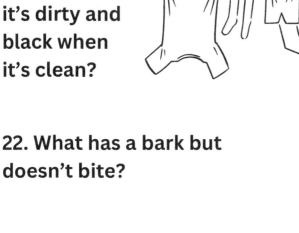

22. What has a bark but doesn't bite?

23. What gets bigger the more you take away from it?

24. What can you catch but not throw?

25. What is so fragile that saying its name breaks it?

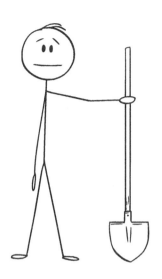

26. I speak without a mouth and hear without ears. I have no body, but I come alive with the wind. What am I?

27. I can be cracked, made, told, and played. What am I?

28. The more you take, the more you leave behind. What am I?

29. What has to be broken before you can use it?

30. I have branches, but no fruit, trunk, or leaves. What am I?

ANSWERS

21. A chalkboard

22. A tree

23. A hole

24. A cold

25. Silence

26. An echo

27. A joke

28. Footsteps

29. An egg

30. A bank

There's a one-story house in which everything is yellow.

Yellow walls,
yellow doors,
yellow furniture.

What colour are the stairs?

There are no stairs

31. What can be broken, but is never held?

32. I am tall when I am young, and I am short when I am old.
What am I?

33. I can fly without wings. I can cry without eyes. Whenever I go, darkness flies. What am I?

34. What has a head, a tail, is brown, and has no legs?

35. What has a heart that doesn't beat?

36. What month of the year has 28 days?

37. What question can you never answer yes to?

38. What can you keep after giving to someone?

39. I shave every day, but my beard stays the same. What am I?

40. The more of this there is, the less you see. What is it?

ANSWERS

31. A promise

36. All of them

32. A candle

37. Are you asleep yet?

33. A cloud

38. Your word

34. A penny

39. A barber

35. An artichoke

40. Darkness

CHALLENGE

Which English word is the odd one out: Stun, Ton, Evil, Letter, Mood, Bad, Strap, Snap, and Straw?

Letter as it is the only one that does not spell another word when it's written backward.

41. What starts with a 'P', ends with an 'E', and has thousands of letters?

42. What word begins with E and ends with E, but only has one letter?

43. What has many rings but no fingers?

44. If you drop a yellow hat in the Red Sea, what does it become?

45. I'm always on the dinner table, but you don't get to eat me. What am I?

46. What goes in a birdbath but never gets wet?

47. What two things can you never eat for breakfast?

48. If you drop me, I'm sure to crack, but smile at me and I'll smile back. What am I?

49. You'll find me in Mercury, Earth, Mars and Jupiter, but not in Venus or Neptune. What am I?

50. Nobody empties me, but I never stay full for long. What am I?

ANSWERS

41. Post office

42. Envelope

43. A telephone

44. Wet

45. Plates and silverware

46. The bird's shadow

47. Lunch and dinner

48. A mirror

49. The letter "R."

50. The moon

CHALLENGE

My first is in chocolate but not in ham. My second is in cake and also in jam. My third at tea time is easily found. Altogether, this is a friend who is often around. What is it?

Cat—"c" is the first letter in "chocolate," "a" is the second letter in "cake" and "jam," and "t" is the third letter in "tea-time.

51. People buy me to eat, but never eat me. What am I?

52. What coat is best put on wet?

53. I have keys, but no locks. I have space, but no room. You can enter, but you can't go outside. What am I?

54. What can you find in a cupboard that can never be put in a saucepan?

55. What's green, but not a leaf, and mimics others, but is not a monkey?

56. What runs around the whole yard without moving?

57. If you have me, you will want to share me. If you share me, you will no longer have me. What am I?

58. What always ends everything?

60. What has words, but never speaks?

59. I'm the rare case when today comes before yesterday. What am I?

ANSWERS

51. Cutlery

56. A fence

52. A coat of paint

57. A secret

53. A computer keyboard

58. The letter G

54. Its lid

59. A dictionary

55. A parrot

60. A book

What is special about the number 854,917,632?

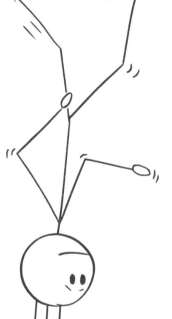

It's the numbers from 1-9 in alphabetical order

61. What kind of band never plays music?

62. If you're running in a race and you pass the person in second place, what place are you in?

63. What can go through glass without breaking it?

64. I have no life, but I can die. What am I?

65. What's black and white and read all over?

66. What is the fastest way to double your money?

67. What has 13 hearts but no other organs?

68. What tastes better than it smells?

69. What goes up and down but doesn't move?

70. What goes through cities and fields, but never moves?

ANSWERS

61. A rubber band

66. Place it in front of the mirror

62. Second place

67. A deck of cards

63. Light

68. Your tongue

64. A battery

69. A staircase

65. A newspaper

70. A road

CHALLENGE

Which will burn longer: the candles on the birthday cake of a boy or the candles on the birthday cake of a girl?

No candles burn longer—
they all burn shorter.

71. I jump when I walk, and sit when I stand. What am I?

72. The alphabet goes from A to Z but I go Z to A.
What am I?

73. Which letter of the alphabet has the most water?

74. My teddy bear is never hungry. Why?

75. What room do ghosts avoid?

76. What kind of tree can you carry in your hand?

77. What building has the most stories?

78. When the water comes down, I go up. What am I?

79. What can you put in a bucket to make it weigh less?

80. How can you drop a raw egg from a height onto a concrete floor without cracking it?

ANSWERS

71. A kangaroo

72. Zebra

73. The letter "c."

74. He's stuffed

75. The living room

76. A palm tree

77. A library

78. An umbrella

79. A hole

80. Concrete floors are very hard to crack.

CHALLENGE

You see a boat filled with people, yet there isn't a single person on board.

How is that possible?

All the people on the boat are married.

81. Why is Europe like a frying pan?

82. When is a door no longer a door?

83. What has four wheels and flies?

84. What starts with T, ends with T, and has T in it?

85. What do the letter "t" and an island have in common?

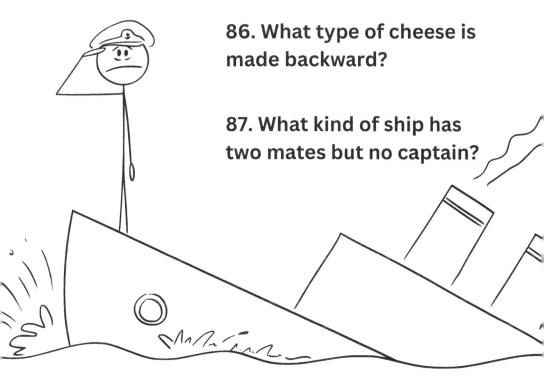

86. What type of cheese is made backward?

87. What kind of ship has two mates but no captain?

88. Who has married many people but has never been married himself?

89. Which word in the dictionary is spelled incorrectly?

90. What do you call a nose that's 12 inches long?

ANSWERS

81. Because it has Greece at the bottom

82. When it's ajar

83. A garbage truck

84. A teapot

85. They're both in the middle of water

86. Edam

87. A relationship

88. A priest

89. Incorrectly

90. A foot

CHALLENGE

Mr. Smith has four daughters. Each of his daughters has a brother.

How many children does Mr. Smith have?

**91. I am easy to lift, but hard to throw.
What am I?**

92. Which fish costs the most?

93. What five-letter word becomes shorter when you add two letters to it?

94. What gets smaller every time it takes a bath?

95. What's always running but never gets hot?

96. Throw away the outside and cook the inside, then eat the outside and throw away the inside. What is it?

97. What 5-letter word typed in all capital letters can be read the same upside down?

98. How do you spell "cow" in thirteen letters?

99. What do you see once in June, twice in November, and not at all in May?

100. What is taken before you can get it?

ANSWERS

91. A feather

92. A goldfish

93. Short

94. Soap

95. A refrigerator

96. Corn on the cob

97. SWIMS

98. SEE O DOUBLE YOU

99. The letter "e."

100. Your picture

CHALLENGE

I am always old, but sometimes also new. While I'm never sad, sometimes I am blue. I am never empty, but only sometimes full. I never push, but I always pull. What am I?

101. What do you throw out when you want to use it but take in when you don't want to use it?

102. What never walks but always runs?

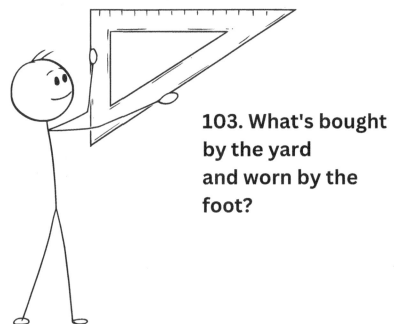

103. What's bought by the yard and worn by the foot?

104. A cowboy rides into town on Friday. He stays three days, then rides out of town on Friday. How?

105. If 2 is company and 3 is a crowd, what are 4 and 5?

106. What can you hold in your right hand, but never in your left hand?

107. A seed with three letters in my name. Take away two and I still sound the same. What am I?

108. Two people are born at the same moment, but they don't have the same birthdays. How?

109. The person who made it doesn't need it. The person who bought it doesn't want it. The person who needs it doesn't know it. What is it?

110. A man goes outside in the rain without an umbrella or hat but doesn't get a single hair on his head wet. How?

ANSWERS

101. An anchor

102. A river

103. A carpet

104. His horse is named Friday

105. 9

106. Your left hand

107. A pea

108. They were born in different time zones

109. A coffin

110. He's bald

CHALLENGE

A man is trapped in a room. The room has only two possible exits: two doors. Through the first door, there is a room constructed from magnifying glasses. The blazing hot sun instantly fries anything or anyone that enters. Through the second door, there is a fire-breathing dragon. How does the man escape?

He waits until night time and then goes through the first door.

111. A bus driver goes the wrong way down a one-way street. He passes the cops, but they don't stop him. Why?

112. I have a head like a cat and feet like a cat, but I am not a cat. What am I?

113. If the day before yesterday was the 23rd, then what will be the day after tomorrow?

114. Whoever makes it doesn't tell. Whoever takes it doesn't know. Whoever knows it doesn't want. What is it?

115. What common English verb becomes its own past tense by rearranging its letters?

116. A is B's father but B isn't A's son. How?

117. What is one thing that all people, regardless of their politics or religion, have to agree is between heaven and earth?

118. I am a protector who sits on a bridge. Only one person can see through me, while others cannot.
What am I?

119. What bats, but never hits; is near a ball, but never thrown?

120. Why did the gardener plant a light bulb in his field?

ANSWERS

111. He was walking

112. A kitten

113. The 27th

114. Counterfeit money

115. Eat

116. B is A's daughter

117. The word "and."

118. Sunglasses

119. Eyelashes

120. He was trying to grow a power plant

CHALLENGE

I am a five-letter word and people eat me. If you remove the first letter I become an energy form. If you remove the first two letters, I am needed to live. Scramble the last three letters and I am a drink. What word am I?

Wheat (heat, eat, tea).

121. I possess a halo of water, walls of stone, and a tongue of wood.
Long I have stood;
what am I?

122. What can run but never walk, have a mouth but never talk, have a head that never weeps, and a bed that never sleeps?

123. If an electric train is moving north at 55 mph and the winds blowing east at 70 mph, which way does the smoke blow?

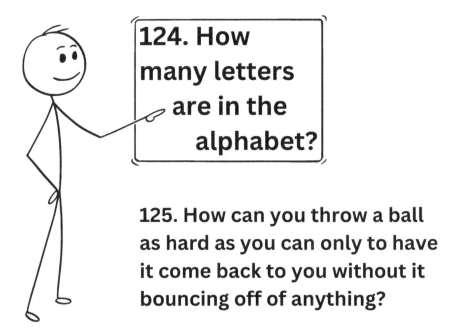

124. How many letters are in the alphabet?

125. How can you throw a ball as hard as you can only to have it come back to you without it bouncing off of anything?

126. What can fill an entire room without taking up any space?

127. The first two letters signify a male, the first three letters signify a female, the first four letters signify a great person, while the entire word signifies a great woman.

128. What has ten letters and starts with gas?

129. People in poverty have this. If you eat this you will die. What is it?

130. What has roots that no one sees and looms much taller than trees? Up it goes but yet it never grows; what is it?

ANSWERS

121. Castle

126. Light

122. A river

127. Heroine

123. An electric train doesn't emit smoke

128. An automobile

124. Eleven letters are in "the alphabet".

129. Nothing

125. Throw the ball straight into the air

130. Mountain

CHALLENGE

Ridley was 11 the day before yesterday, and next year he'll turn 14. How is this possible?

Today is January 1st, and Ridley's birthday is December 31st. Liam was 11 the day before yesterday (December 30th), then turned 12 the next day. This year on December 31st he'll turn 13, so next year he'll turn 14.

131. What is able to go up a chimney when down but unable to go down a chimney when up?

132. If you eat me, my sender will eat you. What am I?

133. Two girls were born to the same mother, on the same day, at the same time, in the same month, and in the same year, however, they're not twins. How is this possible?

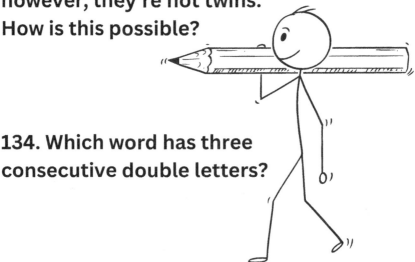

134. Which word has three consecutive double letters?

135. I am born tall and grow short with age. What could I be?

136. The person who makes it and the person who buys it have no use for it and the person who uses it never sees it or feels it. What is it?

137. I promise, I offend, I direct, and I fight. What am I?

138. I fly without wings and cry without eyes. Wherever I lead, darkness follows. What could I be?

139. What is it that no one wants but no one wants to lose?

140. The answer is "yes" but the intent means "no".
What is the question?

ANSWERS

131. An umbrella

132. Fishhook

133. The two girls are a part of a set of triplets

134. Bookkeeper

135. A pencil

136. Coffin

137. A hand

138. A cloud

139. Lawsuit

140. "Do you mind?"

CHALLENGE

Sometimes I am born in silence, Other times, no. I am unseen, But I make my presence known. In time, I fade without a trace. I harm no one, but I am unpopular with all. What am I?

A fart

141. At night they come without being fetched. By day they are lost without being stolen. What are they?

142. What's black when you get it, red when you use it, and white when you're all through with it?

143. You throw away the outside and cook the inside. Then you eat the outside and throw away the inside. What did you eat?

144. All about, but cannot be seen, Can be captured, cannot be held, No throat, but can be heard.

145. Until I am measured I am not known, Yet how you miss me when I have flown.

146. When set loose
I fly away,
Never so cursed
As when I go astray.

147. Lighter than what I am made of,
More of me is hidden
Than is seen.

148. Glittering points
that downward
thrust,
Sparkling spears that
never rust.

149. Three lives have I.
Gentle enough to
soothe the skin,
Light enough to caress
the sky,
Hard enough to crack
rocks.

150. At the sound of me, some may dream
or stamp their feet,
At the sound of me, some may laugh
or sometimes weep.

ANSWERS

141. The stars

146. A fart

142. Charcoal

147. Iceberg

143. An ear of corn

148. Icicle

144. Wind

149. Water

145. Time

150. Music

CHALLENGE

A clerk in a butcher shop stands 5'10" and wears size 13 shoes.

What does he weigh?

Meat

151. I build up castles.
I tear down mountains.
I make some men blind,
I help others to see.
What am I?

152. Two in a corner, 1 in a room,
0 in a house, but 1 in a shelter.
What am I

153. How far will a blind dog walk into a forest?

154. What happens when you throw a yellow rock into a purple stream?

155.
You saw me where I never was and where I could not be. And yet within that very place, my face you often see.
What am I?

156. What is it that after you take away the whole, some still remains?

157. A box without hinges, lock or key, yet golden treasure lies within.
What is it?

158. Forward I'm heavy, but backwards I'm not.
What am I?

159. I can be long, or I can be short.
I can be grown, and I can be bought.
I can be painted, or left bare.
I can be round, or square.
What am I?

160. Kings and queens may cling to power and the jester's got his call,
But, as you may all discover, the common one outranks them all.

ANSWERS

151. Sand

156. Wholesome

152. The letter r

157. An egg

153. Halfway. After he gets halfway, he's walking out of the forest.

158. Ton

154. It makes a splash

159. A fingernail

155. A reflection

160. An ace (in a deck of cards)

CHALLENGE

As I was going to St. Ives, I met a man with seven wives; each wife had seven sacks; each sack had seven cats; each cat had seven kits; kits, cats, sacks, and wives. How many were there going to St. Ives?"

161. What kind of cup doesn't hold water?

162. What two keys can't open any door?

163. A man and his boss have the same parents but are not siblings. How is this possible?

164. It's red, blue, purple and green, no one can reach it, not even the queen. What is it?

165. I am so simple that I can only point, yet I guide people all over the world

166. I am not alive, but I grow; I don't have lungs, but I need air. What am I?

167. What is easier to get into than out of?

168. Remove my skin and I won't cry, but you might!

169. A man looks at a painting and says, "Brothers and sisters I have none, but that man's father is my father's son." Who is in the painting?

170. I am taken from a mine, and shut up in a wooden case, from which I am never released, and yet I am used by almost every person. What am I?

ANSWERS

161. A cupcake

162. A monkey and a donkey

163. He's self-employed

164. A rainbow

165. Compass

166. A balloon

167. Trouble

168. An onion

169. His son

170. Pencil lead

CHALLENGE

A man who was outside in the rain without an umbrella or hat didn't get a single hair on his head wet. Why?

He was bald

171. Almost everyone needs it, asks for it, and gives it, but almost nobody takes it. What is it?

172. A man was driving a black truck. His lights were not on. The moon was not out. A lady was crossing the street. How did the man see her?

173. If six children and two dogs were under an umbrella, how come none of them got wet?

174. A man and a dog were going down the street. The man rode, yet walked. What was the dog's name?

175. Thousands lay up gold within this house, but no man-made it. Spears past counting guard this house, but no man wards it.

176. Why did Snap, Crackle, and Pop get scared?

177. Why is an island like the letter T?

178. What has wheels and flies, but it is not an aircraft?

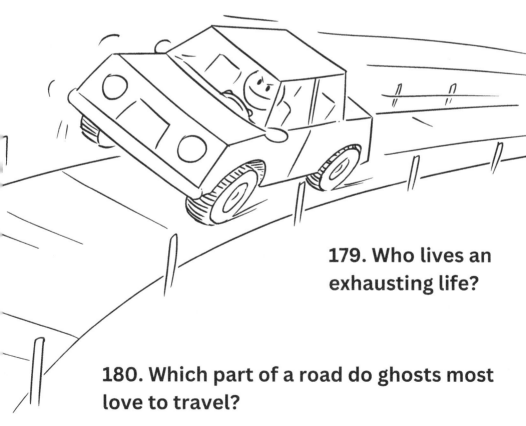

179. Who lives an exhausting life?

180. Which part of a road do ghosts most love to travel?

ANSWERS

171. Advice

172. It was a bright, sunny day.

173. Because it wasn't raining

174. Yet

175. Beehive

176. They heard there was a cereal killer on the loose

177. They're both in the middle of water!

178. A garbage truck

179. The exhaust

180. The dead end

CHALLENGE

A man went to the hardware store to buy
items for his house.
1 would cost $.25
12 would cost $.50
122 would cost $.75
When he left the store he had spent $.75,
what did he buy?

House numbers

181. What has many teeth but can't bite?

182. What has legs but cannot walk?

183. What can kids make but never see?

184. What comes out at night without being called, and is lost in the day without being stolen?

185. What is made of water, but if you put it into water it vanishes?

186. What kind of lion never roars?

187. What can you serve that you cannot eat?

188. I grow down as I grow up. What am I?

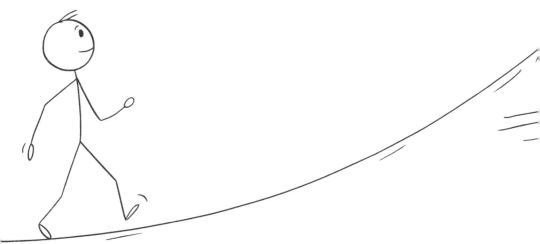

189. What's black, white and blue?

190. What has a thousand needles but cannot sew?

ANSWERS

181. A zipper

186. A dandelion

182. A chair

187. A tennis ball

183. Noise

188. A goose. Goose feathers are called down

184. The stars

189. A sad zebra

185. An ice cube

190. A porcupine

CHALLENGE

A rooster is sitting on the roof of a barn facing west. If it laid an egg, would the egg roll to the north or to the south?

It's impossible — roosters don't lay eggs.

191. Why can't a pirate ever finish the alphabet?

192. What do you answer even though it never asks you questions?

193. Strip the skin under my skin, and my flesh you'll reveal. It tastes sweet and tart, now throw out the peel. What is it?

194. Which of the following is the largest? Triangle, circle, square, or rectangle?

195. Break it and it gets better; set it and it's harder to break

196. You have me today, Tomorrow you'll have more; As your time passes, I'm not easy to store; I don't take up space, But I'm only in one place; I am what you saw, But not what you see. What am I?

197. If two snakes marry, what will their towels say?

198. On Christmas Eve, when Santa leaves his workshop at the North Pole, what direction does he travel?

199. What four-letter word ends in it and can be found at the bottom of birdcages?

200. People make me, save me, change me, raise me. What am I?

ANSWERS

191. Because he always gets lost at sea!

196. Memories

192. A doorbell or a phone

197. Hiss and hers

193. Orange

198. South. The only way to travel from the North Pole is south.

194. Rectangle, it has the most letters

199. Grit

195. Record

200. Money

CHALLENGE

Four cars come to a four-way stop, each coming from a different direction. They can't decide who got there first, so they all go forward at the same time. All 4 cars go, but none crash into each other. How is this possible?

They all turned the same way - right (USA) or left (UK)

201. What walks all day on its head?

202. When does Christmas come before Thanksgiving?

203. I have a head like a cat and feet like a cat, but I am not a cat. What am I?

204. What's orange and sounds like a parrot?

205. What do you call it when your parachute doesn't open?

206. You cannot come in or go out without me. What am I?

207. I am hard like stone, but I grow on your body. What am I?

208. What goes up and down the stairs without moving?

209. I can be long, or I can be short. I can be grown, or I can be bought. I can be painted or left bare. I can be round, or square. What am I?

210. I shrink smaller every time I take a bath. What am I?

ANSWERS

201. A nail in a horseshoe

206. A door

202. In the dictionary

207. A tooth

203. A kitten

208. A carpet

204. A carrot

209. A fingernail

205. Jumping to a conclusion

210. Soap

CHALLENGE

Two fathers and two sons went fishing one day. They were there the whole day and only caught three fish. One father said, "that is enough for all of us. We will have one each." How can that be possible?

There were only three men. The grandfather was fishing with his son and grandson.

211. A precious stone, as clear as diamond. Seek it out while the sun's near the horizon. Though you can walk on water with its power, try to keep it, and it'll vanish in an hour.

212. What cruel person would sit on a baby?

213. What is a weighty currency?

214. Some are used for fabric, some are used for hair, some are used for paper and one is called a pair

215. I am always running, but never get tired or hot. What am I?

216. How many bananas can you eat if your stomach is empty?

217. What falls often but never gets hurt?

218. I can travel at nearly 100 miles per hour, but never leave the room. You can cover me up, but that doesn't slow me down. You will not know if I come only once or again and again and again. What am I?

219. I like to twirl my body but keep my head up high. After I go in, everything becomes tight. What am I?

220. Turn me on my side and I am everything. Cut me in half and I am nothing. What am I?

ANSWERS

211. Ice

216. Just one after that it's not empty anymore.

212. Babysitter

217. Snow or rain

213. A pound

218. A sneeze

214. Scissors

219. Screw

215. The refrigerator

220. The number 8 on its side

CHALLENGE

You walk into a room that contains a match, a kerosene lamp, a candle and a fireplace. What would you light first?

The match

221. What seven-letter word becomes longer when the third letter is removed?

222. What is red and smells like paint?

223. What is bought by the yard by is worn by the foot?

224. What has a foot but no leg?

225. What stays where it is when it goes off?

226. What has a big mouth, yet never speaks?

**227. It's shorter than the rest, but when you're happy, you raise it up like it's the best.
What is it?**

228. What water can you eat and chew?

229. What can you fill with empty hands?

230. What moves across the land but never has to steer? It has delivered our goods year after year. What is it?

ANSWERS

221. Lounger = Longer

226. Jar

222. Red paint

227. Thumb

223. Carpet

228. Watermelon

224. Ruler

229. Gloves

225. Alarm clock

230. Train

CHALLENGE

What 8 letter word can have a letter taken away and it still makes a word. Take another letter away and it still makes a word. Keep on doing that until you have one letter left. What is the word?

The word is starting! starting, staring, string, sting, sing, sin, in, I

231. What has golden hair and stands in the corner?

232. My rings are not of gold, but I get more as I get old.
What am I?

233. I beam, I shine, I sparkle white.
I'll brighten the day with a single light.
I'll charm and enchant all.
I'll bring the best in you all.
What am I?

234. Tickle with your fingers and a song it will sing. Be careful, though, you may break a string.
What is it?

235. What do pandas have that no other animal has?

236. What is it that no person ever saw, which never was, but always will be?

237. I go around and in the house, but never touches the house.
What am I?

238. I am known for my natural tuxedo and marching. What am I?

239. What can you lose that will cause other people to lose theirs too?

240. I can be flipped and broken but I never move. I can be closed, and opened, and sometimes removed. I am sealed by hands. What am I?

ANSWERS

231. A broom

236. Tomorrow

232. A tree

237. Sun

233. Smile

238. A penguin

234. Guitar

239. Temper

235. Baby pandas

240. A deal

CHALLENGE

What is the longest word in the dictionary?

241. What is deaf, dumb and blind but always tells the truth?

242. What word looks the same upside down and backward?

243. I have two legs, but they only touch the ground while I'm at rest.
What am I?

244. The more you take, the more you leave behind. What am I?

245. What must take a bow before it can speak?

246. Different lights do make me strange, thus into different sizes I will change. What am I?

247. My thunder comes before the lightning;
My lightning comes before the clouds;
My rain dries all the land it touches.
What am I?

248. You can see me in water, but I never get wet. What am I?

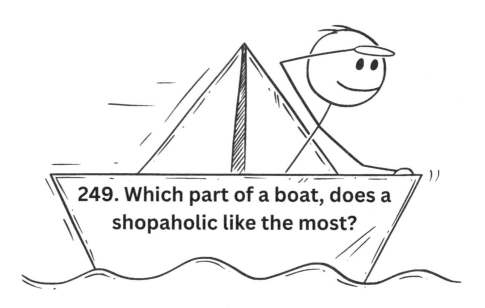

249. Which part of a boat, does a shopaholic like the most?

250. I have no feet, no hands, no wings, but I climb to the sky. What am I?

ANSWERS

241. A mirror

246. I am the pupil of an eye.

242. SWIMS

247. A volcano

243. Wheelbarrow

248. A reflection

244. Fingerprints

249. The sail

245. Violin

250. Smoke

CHALLENGE

How can you write down eight eights so that they add up to one thousand?

251. Which word is least like the others? Third, fourth, fifth, sixth, seventh, eighth, ninth?

252. What is the last thing you take off before bed?

253. What is 3/7 chicken, 2/3 cat, and 2/4 goat?

254. What invention allows people to look right through a wall?

255. What would you find in the middle of Toronto?

256. If two's a company and three's a crowd, what are four and five?

257. Which is heavier: a ton of bricks or a ton of feathers?

258. A girl goes to the store and buys one dozen eggs. As she walks home, all but three break. How many eggs are left unbroken?

259. What five-letter word has one left when two are removed?

260. What has many eyes but is unable to see?

ANSWERS

251. Third, it is the only one not ending in "th".

256. Nine

252. Your feet from the floor!

257. Neither because they both weigh a ton

253. Chicago!

258. Three

254. A window

259. Stone

255. The letter "o"

260. A potato

CHALLENGE

You walk into a creepy house by yourself. There is no electricity, plumbing, or ventilation.

Inside you notice 3 doors with numbers on them. Once you open the doors you will suffer the consequence.

Door #1 You'll be eaten by a lion who is hungry.

Door #2 You'll be trapped forever.

Door #3 There is an electric chair waiting for you. Which door do you pick?

Door #3, since there is no electricity to harm you.

261. I have one head, one foot, and four legs. What am I?

262. How do you share 21 apples between 20 people?

263. When is a door no longer a door?

264. What is put on the table and cut. but never eaten?

265. What breaks but never falls and falls but never breaks?

266. What are the next three letters in this combination: OTTFFSS?

267. First, think of the color of clouds. Next, think of the color of snow. Now, think of the color of a full bright moon. What do cows drink?

268. I am never scared but became petrified and can't live in a house but would die to make one. What am I?

269. It has five wheels though often thought of as four but you cannot use it without that one more. What is it?

270. My thunder comes before the lightning; my lightning comes before clouds; my rain dries all the land it touches. What am I?

ANSWERS

261. A bed

266. E N T (eight, nine, and ten).

262. Make apple sauce

267. Water

263. When it's ajar

268. A tree

264. A pack of cards

269. A car

265. Day and night

270. A volcano

CHALLENGE

What was the biggest island in the world before the discovery of Greenland?

Greenland was always the biggest—people just didn't know it yet.

271. How high do you have to count before you use the letter "a" in the English spelling of the whole number?

272. What's mine that only you can have?

273. What time is it when an elephant sits on a fence?

274. A king, a queen, and two twins all lay in a large room. How are there no adults in the room?

275. What five-letter word stays the same when you take away the first, third, and last letter?

276. You always find me in the past, I can be created in the present, but the future can never taint me. What am I?

277. What can go up a chimney down, but can't go down a chimney up?

278. A monkey, a squirrel, and a bird are racing to the top of a coconut tree. Who gets to the banana first? Is it the monkey, the squirrel, or the bird?

279. When you look for something, why is it always in the last place you look?

280. If you multiply me by any other number, the answer will always remain the same. What number am I?

ANSWERS

271. One thousand

276. History

272. My heart

277. An umbrella

273. It's time to fix the fence

278. There are no bananas at the top of a coconut tree!

274. They're all beds!

279. Because when you find it, you stop looking!

275. Empty

280. 0

MAKE YOUR OWN RIDDLE

PART ONE

1. Start with the answer

Come up with the solution to your riddle first, then work backwards to create your question. Your solution can be almost anything, but choosing a physical object is an easy way to start.

Ex. The answer to my riddle is "carrot."

2. Brainstorm

Write down any words or phrases that could be associated with your answer.

Consider:

Synonyms

Similar things

Things it does

Features it has

How to describe it

Ex. Carrots are orange with green leaves on top.

281. What has no beginning, end, or middle?

282. A girl is sitting in a house at night that has no lights on at all. There is no lamp, no candle, nothing. Yet she is reading. How?

283. What is next in this sequence? JFMAMJJASON . . .

284. How can a man go 8 days without sleep?

285. Five pieces of coal, a carrot, and a scarf are lying on the lawn. Nobody put them on the lawn but there is a perfectly logical reason why they should be there. What is it?

286. I possess a halo of water, walls of stone, and a tongue of wood. Long I have stood; what am I?

287. There are 6 sisters. Each sister has 1 brother. How many brothers are in the sister's family?

288. A man runs away from home, turns left three times, and ends up back at home facing a man in a mask. Who is wearing the mask?

289. When does 11+3=2?

290. Which is correct: 18 plus 19 is 36. Or 18 plus 19 are 36?

ANSWERS

281. A doughnut

286. Castle

282. The woman is blind and is reading braille

287. 1 brother

283. The letter "D." The sequence contains the first letter of each month.

288. The man in the mask is a catcher because this is a game of baseball

284. He only sleeps at night

289. On a clock

285. Remains of a melted snowman

290. Actually, both are incorrect – 18 plus 19 is 37!

MAKE YOUR OWN RIDDLE
PART TWO

3. Think like your answer
If your answer were a person, what would they think? What would they do? How would they describe themselves? How would they see the world around them?

Ex. If I were a carrot, I might think I was wearing a green hat.

4. Think outside the sentence
Use figurative language — like a metaphor, simile, personification or hyperbole — to make comparisons or describe your answer in new ways. This is often what makes the riddle tricky for the reader to solve.

Ex. A carrot sounds like "a parrot."

291. What has two humps and is found at the North Pole?

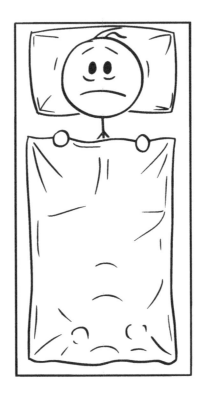

292. During which month do people sleep the least?

293. What's the capital of France?

294. What can jump higher than a building?

295. How do you fix a damaged jack-o-lantern?

296. It spends most of its day eating white, but when it's quick enough, it gets to eat fruit and sometimes some blue things. It's in a dark room, where the walls are blue, it runs from a ghost that roams the halls and haunts it all the time. What is it?

297. What comes down but never goes up?

298. I went into the woods and got it, I sat down to seek it, I brought it home with me because I couldn't find it.

299. What vehicle is spelled the same backwards and forwards?

300. I'm a god, a planet, and I measure heat. What am I?

ANSWERS

291. A lost camel!

292. February (There are fewer days!)

293. The letter "F." It's the only capital letter in France

294. Anything that can jump — buildings don't jump, silly!

295. You use a pumpkin patch

296. Pac-Man

297. Rain

298. A splinter

299. Racecar

300. Mercury

MAKE YOUR OWN RIDDLE
PART THREE

5. Write your riddle!
Now that you have the backbone of your riddle, the only thing left to do is write! Use clear, descriptive language to write out your riddle, then share it with friends and family to see if they can solve it.

If you want to show your riddle in a different way, you could even think about presenting it as a pun, like a knock-knock joke! Or if you're looking to make a really tricky riddle or a brain teaser, you could use something visual like a deck of cards.

Ex. I'm orange, wear a green hat and sound like a parrot. What am I?
A carrot!

Made in the USA
Las Vegas, NV
04 January 2025